LUNATIC ENGINE

LUNATIC ENGINE

PAUL PEARSON

TURNSTONE PRESS

Lunatic Engine
copyright © Paul Pearson 2020
Turnstone Press
Artspace Building
206-100 Arthur Street
Winnipeg, MB
R3B 1H3 Canada
www.TurnstonePress.com

Turnstone Press gratefully acknowledges the assistance of the Canada Council
for the Arts, the Manitoba Arts Council, the Government of Canada through the
Canada Book Fund, and the Province of Manitoba through the Book Publishing
Tax Credit and the Book Publisher Marketing Assistance Program.

Excerpt(s) from GALILEO'S DAUGHTER by Dava Sobel, Copyright
© 1999 Dava Sobel. Reprinted by permission Viking Canada, a division
of Penguin Random House Canada Limited. All rights reserved.

Epigraph pg xi is from *Science*. "Instructions for Preparing an Initial Manuscript."
Accessed November 21, 2019. https://www.sciencemag.org/authors/instructions-
preparing-initial-manuscript. Reprinted with permission from AAAS.

Cover: PIA01384: Jupiter's Great Red Spot. Image credit: NASA/JPL; image
addition date: 1998-12-05.

Printed and bound in Canada.

Library and Archives Canada Cataloguing in Publication

Title: Lunatic engine / Paul Pearson.
Names: Pearson, Paul, 1970- author.
Description: Poems.
Identifiers: Canadiana (print) 2019023329X | Canadiana (ebook)
    20190233303 | ISBN 9780888016935 (softcover)
    | ISBN 9780888016942 (EPUB) | ISBN 9780888016959 (Kindle)
    | ISBN 9780888016966 (PDF)
Classification: LCC PS8531.E29 L86 2020 | DDC C811/.6—dc23

MANITOBA ARTS COUNCIL
CONSEIL DES ARTS DU MANITOBA

Canada Council   Conseil des arts
for the Arts   du Canada

Funded by the Government of Canada
Financé par le gouvernement du Canada | Canada

Manitoba

MIX
Paper from
responsible sources
FSC
www.fsc.org   FSC® C103567

To Suzanne, my fixed centre

CONTENTS

(OR MOVE WITHIN IT)

ABSTRACT

*Abstracts of Research Articles and Reports should explain to
the general reader why the research was done, what was found
and why the results are important. They should start with some
brief BACKGROUND information: a sentence giving a broad
introduction to the field comprehensible to the general reader,
and then a sentence of more detailed background specific to
your study. This should be followed by an explanation of the
OBJECTIVES/METHODS and then the RESULTS. The final
sentence should outline the main CONCLUSIONS of the study,
in terms that will be comprehensible to all our readers.*

—American Association for the Advancement of Science

Introduction: Themes for Book Club

[I]nviting the attention of all who are eager for true philosophy to the beginnings which led to the sight of most important phenomena.

—Galileo

1. The relationship with your father, stargazer, absent parent.
2. The death of your mother.
3. The love poems, your relationship with your spouse.
4. Becoming a father (and the deep concern that you'll do it right).
5. The mirror world of Galileo and his daughter—another complex but loving relationship.
6. The drive to understand the universe, then and now, given the tools we have.

METHODS: SOURCES AND FOOTNOTES

Let us not then despise those Hints, though very dark, which
Reason, after some contemplation, offereth to our Intelligence ....

—Galileo

This book owes an enormous debt to Dava Sobel, whose books introduced me to the words of Galileo and his daughter, Suor Maria Celeste—a dialogue between science and religion that echoes through the centuries, and which I found I wanted to take part in. Their words became chapter headings in Sobel's book, *Galileo's Daughter,* and these chapter headings in turn became the titles for the poems in the first section of this book, "Bodies That Stay Atop Water."

The titles of Galileo's own books became the titles of poems in the last section of this work, "Bibliography."

So my own poems became responses to a conversation that began long ago. Other fragments of writing by Galileo and Suor Maria Celeste were pulled from another of Dava Sobel's books, *Letters to Father.* They became the source for all the lines in "As I Struggle to Understand" and "In the Chambers of the Holy Office of the Inquisition."

Throughout the first section, you'll see footnotes, which are also fragments from the letters between Galileo and his daughter—as if they were commenting on phrases in this book. The conversation continues in the second section, "(or move within it)," where I have assembled the footnotes into one poem and the phrases they refer to in a second. You are invited to continue this conversation by arranging these fragments in other ways on the blank pages of poems "3" and "4."

RESULTS AND CONCLUSION: DIALOGUE
CONCERNING THE TWO CHIEF WORLD SYSTEMS

For the invisible things of him from the creation of the world are clearly seen, being understood by the things that are made, even his eternal power and Godhead; so that they are without excuse
....

—Romans 1:20

In consequence of this that hath been demonstrated, sundry and various Conclusions may be gathered, by which the truth of my principall Proposition comes to be more and more confirmed....

—Galileo

In the winter of 1999, Suzanne gave me a book. We had only been married for a little over a year and were still in the hesitant stage of giving each other spontaneous gifts, still exploring each other's coastlines. But we had a shared sense that there was no horizon to our future and we were both possessed with an insatiable appetite to learn the secrets of the universe. *Galileo's Daughter* was a fitting choice.

It was early December and I was hiding out in the staff residence at Emerald Lake Lodge. Sue had finished her first year of culinary school and was picking up some extra cash and kitchen experience. We were young enough that being apart for two weeks was impossible.

Tucked up at the top of Yoho National Park, the lodge was nearly buried in snow, making it difficult to go outside. Daylight all but disappeared beneath the snow and clouds and while everyone else worked, I was utterly alone for hours on end. As darkness set in, it was just me, a million trees, forty feet of pure white snow, and an infinite night sky lousy with stars. And silence. Yes, don't forget the silence.

And so I found myself alone with Dava Sobel's book, overflowing with every sort of poetic trope a young writer could want. Galileo, the father of the experimental method, the first modern man, and his illegitimate daughter both confined—she to the convent, he under house arrest by the Inquisition—and mortally limited by the Church. Sue and I both have Catholic backgrounds—hers French, mine Italian. But as soon as we were both allowed to decide for ourselves, we both chose to have nothing to do with the Catholics, or any Christian church for that matter. At all. Full stop. And yet here I was captured by something so Catholic and yet, somehow not. A story of filial love and devotion, lemon sweets and telescopes, domestic finance, fear and Judgment. The very stuff of both science and poetry lay in my open hands.

Then there were those chapter titles. Who could resist phrases like "She who was so precious to you," "What we require above all else," and "As I struggle to understand"? The poems almost write themselves. Indeed, the two italicized ones in this collection did. A couple of the poems also go off in their own surprising little directions, like "That I Should Be Begged to Publish Such a Work" and "She Who Was So Precious to You," a poem I wrote for Suzanne early in our relationship after visiting her mother's gravesite. Some of the poems foreshadowed others.

The book you hold in your hands came together slowly over the course of a much-interrupted decade. I do not need to describe all the delays and peregrinations that came next, the cul-de-sacs, dead ends, pits and valleys. Somewhere in all of this was a transition. Somewhere we stopped being young newlyweds. Somewhere we stopped being angry at our upbringing. Maybe it was Galileo, maybe it was the poetry. Maybe it was the kids, the garden, the funerals, the crushing routine boredom. Or maybe it was trying to figure out how I would answer the questions my children will inevitably ask. I will say that I am happy that this collection does not end where it began.

So back in the snow at Emerald Lake, I was holding what I thought to be a book of answers. It turned out to be as treacherous as all books are and became a book of questions in my hands, asking me: What do you value? What are you striving for? Does the endless, repetitive minutiae of daily life mean anything? What will you stand for? Who will be the witness? How have we as a species survived? Why can't we see that we have too many different words for the same concepts?—of course the Tower of Babel confused all of our names for God. Did you really think that there was a difference between science and religion? What do you believe?

What am I going to tell my kids? What am I going to tell them about what they hold in their hands? What we've left them?

we just figured out evolution a century and a half ago
yet some still deny we're cooking ourselves in our
own atmosphere because we're clever enough to suck
combustibles out of the ground but too stupid to stop
burning
everything
and the memory of my newborn son
clenched up in the bath like a fist
red and scared
is burned into my being

this is where it either all comes together
or all falls apart specific and the universal
looking through the iced-over part of the window
kept up by the cat howling all night
carrying a stuffed pink bear around
like a kitten
or a dead bird
these poems all trailing
off like a lost thought
a sentence of sorts

Galileo's *Dialogues* banned
for two dogmatic centuries
my father was an understanding man

and he barely ever spoke

three years later my daughter
clenched up red and scared
in the same tub as her brother
the same fist

Galileo's daughter read of her father's disgrace
before the Inquisition in the convent
of San Matteo cloistered
and powerless

I'm having a bit of difficulty this morning
I've been trying to write this for hours
but the realization that I'm an orphan
has struck me dumb

what am I going to tell them about the motion
of the earth the stability of the sun the order
of the heavens and the arrangements of the
        celestial spheres
what am I going to tell them here at the
continually unravelling end?

the simplest act
bathing my children
washing their feet

displacement

LUNATIC ENGINE

BODIES THAT
STAY ATOP WATER

Therefore, beginning to investigate with the examination of exquisite Experiments ....

—Galileo

Bodies That Stay Atop Water

or don't
move without it or
move
without remembering or
remember
when movement didn't rely on
memory
moves
water and bodies
to write books about water and memory
moves
this body from city and science
and our bodies to the bush and its bodies
and its past and its
god
it is
so many bodies so much memory
moving like water or so much
water moving over bodies
of memory bodies moving within bodies
that stay within memory or
move atop
it or

fuck it
baby

let's just start this let's just
get married against our mothers' wishes and have
miscarriages and have kids and be good mothers and
fathers and get jobs and buy houses and buy cats and
bury cats and bury mothers and ignore signs and deny
sorrows and
see who
floats and who
doesn't

SHE WHO WAS SO PRECIOUS TO YOU
for Suzanne, and the mother-in-law I never met

though your hands are sometimes
granite in my hands
so long since the marker
was placed and settled the suburbs
are swallowing the cemetery the city
is holding our dead in its mouth
and you are holding your dead
in your blood her voice rings
in your ears the mother whose memory
I hear in your words[1-30] whose loss I see
in your sleep curled up here in the clamorous heart
of the city

1–30 *since we are all of us here on Earth like strangers*

the aerodynamics of eyelash
and blink
leaves caught in a gust
a burst
of dreaming

the mathematics of sleep on
your face small wrinkles
relaxing to their lowest
common denominator
laugh lines
leaving

streetlight gauze softening
the minutes, the seconds, the slow
arc of time describing
the clumsy circumference
of the heart

god, Alden was right
we're all maudlin boobs
I'm here watching you sleep trying
to compare your hair to
the moon's penumbra[2-5] a vague
ring around the language I learned from
my father's books

2–5 *I think you will be much pleased with it*

before we take this trip
let's agree to be careful
to not let our imaginations run away
to remember
this story
can only go one page at a time

BRIGHT STARS SPEAK OF YOUR VIRTUES

speak of light pollution
    and of smog
speak of the night sky club
    campaigning for cowls on streetlights
speak of how we don't look
    up anymore because there's nothing
    to see but a few fixed stars
    a satellite
speak of the moon
    and its forgotten faces
    our ignorance
    of tides
speak of how we don't
    go there anymore
speak of this highway
    alone so
    many stars my eye
    can't hold them all
speak of my father[3-17] on a ridge
    my ten-year-old skin
    shivering the constellations
    crackling their stubborn
    refusal to look like their names to look
    like the illustrations in my book my skin
    can't stop

3–17 *could drink in this universal power and authority*

speak of his unfailing ability to identify
    Taurus, Libra,
    Cancer
    my mind can't hold them all
speak of his unfailing inability to identify
    anything earthbound
    any of us
speak of anything but
    the stars in the city
    only the brightest
    for the rest
    nothing

To Have the Truth Seen and Recognized

sideways six hours
from noon this light this late
fall sunset lasts half
the day driving home
from the foothills

to the careless eye
everything is brown but
smaller spectrums catch
the sun's push through thickening
prairie air in tricks of gold amber
copper

in the city
I don't see the sun[4-27]
all light is street
light interstitial and weak
wired with a switch

between the binaries I've never
seen the red in your hair so
clearly

4–27 *this rule is never broken*

the first draft of this was an imagined account of the
teenager next-door's death by driving too fast down the
dump road the late afternoon sun flashing on the nearly
still beaver-dammed creek just off the shoulder a sharp
turn taken over undercut gravel crumbling and the old
truck is on its side

water pouring into the cab from below sun pouring in
from above

the second draft of this was all about the science the
immutability of the heavens the immobility of the Earth
Galileo and the Nova of 1604 the true word of God an
authority even higher than the Bible

Copernicus pulled the pin on the heliocentric grenade
then promptly died before it could go off

Galileo picked it up tested its weight through math
and motion even before his telescope and his satellites
holding that grenade in the very face of the sun and its
spots its clouds its vapours attracted from the aether

when you get to the end of all of this you'll look back and
know this is the point

the quality of miracles isn't what it used to be[5-20]

caught between the metonymy of dump roads and grenades
and the memory of your first childhood encounter with death
you're sitting suspended immobilized
the mutable sun blinding you
as the immutable waters rise

5–20 *obliging me to hide in silence*

this is the first two body problem
a daughter of God and the father of science separated
what Galileo's eye augmented by bending
light to curiosity, Maria Celeste bent to augment
God's alchemy and the mathematics of prayer
there is no mortar
without pestle

our half-lives here are anointed
by the traffic of right angles and roundabouts
aneled by the quantum mechanics of steel and speed
our faith is ground, tubed, and focused into a resolution
twenty times clearer than
the wisdom of the patriarchs degrades[6-15]
by God's will the distance is dying

you say all of this to me as we drive out
as we leave our present towards my past
my own private bush of ghosts
we drive at night to see the stars
the Milky Way smudges our path across the sky
along the plane of the ecliptic there is
a catching up, a retrograde of orbits
as we leave Mars behind navigate by Jupiter

6–15 *seeing the splendor of the sun and the stars*

I am enraptured by she who was cloistered
captured by he who was confined
by the same God by the same
will the spirit is literally moving us
bound to this trajectory will you be strong enough
will I

memory acting at a distance
equals speed times my
time in the bush of ghosts
is not no matter how far
away I get it's not
done

burn all the forests down
flood every city I've lived
in crumble it all back
to the Stone Age take away
agriculture and stone knives
rub out this crude cave painting
I could be a monkey[7-26]
in a tree and there'd still be
enough past to pull my orbit
apart

give me the coelacanth
the trilobite the primordial
muck give me anything but ...

7-26 *by living in obedience / without anything of one's own / and in chastity*

CONJECTURE HERE AMONG SHADOWS

… let me offer you an explanation:

my mother disappeared for a month when
I was ten she had to go to the hospital
my father said she needed operating
on her insides were broken but she'd be
okay and back in a month and for a
month he quit
drinking

Mrs. Tycho the librarian said the part
of my mother that made babies was
broken Mrs. Tycho spelled hysterectomy
out for my inquiring mind and he quit
drinking

a month of Hungry-Man my brother
and I eating from TV trays on the black and white
bridge of the Enterprise in our living
room dad sat in his
La-Z-Boy we were Sulu and Chekov
a sober Captain Kirk behind us

and our mother did get better and she did
come home and they cancelled *Star Trek*
and   and
and

lying here with my hand on
your soon-to-be-swelling belly waiting[8-10]
for our first child for the second
time I'm scared that part of you
that part of me is broken that part
of us is about to be
cancelled

8–10 *until there shall be given to us the true / constitution of the*
parts of the universe

How Our Father is Favoured

by the beating wings of wasps
we must *patiently*

by the split syrinx of songbirds
we must *submit*

by the friction of water on stone
we must *ourselves*

by the striking and scraping of chitin
we must *will*

by this experience[9-2] we know but a few
methods for making sounds
by this endless fractal expansion of knowledge
we must patiently submit ourselves to the will

9-2 *he was sure that many more existed / which were not only*
unknown / but unimaginable

To Busy Myself in Your Service

this is what it means
to be a fat her
to pick
up aft her
you puke and mewl in the mornings
to be so sick from such joy
is back
words get
made up[10-3] the bed
for you I wash
the floors do all the dishes to be
a fat her is to
be broke in
things drop but
I pick them up things delay
but eventually get done I learn short
cuts but this is too much
you watch
football your pants un
done
a bag of ketchup chips lies empty
on the couch beside you baby likes ketchup
chips you smile red face smear sticky fingers wave
at my armload of clothes now move you're in
my way & the Vikings are thrashing the Packers

10–3 *so beautifully written / that they have only kindled / my desire to see more*

I iron in an
other room marvel at the in
side out of things now Vikings
thrash
the Packers?

I think it's going to be
a boy

WHAT WE REQUIRE ABOVE ALL ELSE

Is a not her poem
about s no w
about the negat ives in
side every thing a s now flake too
is built around an ab sence
a little hole you can put
stuff in to a word a tiny
knife hard voice I m sure
that time he said that
me an thing (or the time s he did not say any thing) no
no t the memory but the time it self
will fit in side one of those small white holes[11-25]
un less they have all been filled al ready
where then will you put all
the things that could fill the who le
of you what we re quire the n a bove all els e is mo
re s n o w

[11-25] *who appreciate the true significance of their calling*

cause we've dropped the be
a new fetish[12-6] for short
words because be
comes less an
aphora and more
an un spoken ex
cause human
bodies are bad at re
producing our desires   still
lurk be tween the sheets
cause missed carriages only
happen to other heroines   still
in a Victorian sense the in
ability to be three
from two leaves us   still
minus one cause we had
to be better at being
parents than our parents   still
waiting for a grand   still
child to be still not be
still be still be
still

12-6 *though I know that your joy must be / tainted with consid-erable sorrow*

THROUGH MY MEMORY OF THEIR ELOQUENCE

in the third trimester
your hands
vein and swell
like tree swallows[13-4]
swelling into clouds or
a chorus of frogs
stuttering in the distance
growing concordant as the night
settles and rests
like tree swallows
or your two hands
through their eloquence
I shall know grace
through my memory of their eloquence

13–4 *an extraordinary thing in this cold season*

A SMALL AND TRIFLING BODY
for Oscar

should not have taken so much
         blood to wash itself out
should not have torn
        her keel in two

10 lbs of potatoes	=	easy to deliver
10 lbs of flour	=	easy to deliver
10 lbs of cocaine	=	easy to deliver
10 lbs of baby	=	knotted and clenched
		stuck
		like a fist in a mouth[14–33]

not such a small
body after all not
such a trifle to
hold your little blue
body her body blue
veined and open
wide uterus lies
like a tongue on
her thighs her in
sides spoke you
out while it

14–33 *I fear this activity will do you harm*

is all I can
do to stand
struck dumb
and speech
less

semi	;	colon
con	;	junction
what's my	;	function
son to my father	;	father to my son
broke a silence	;	took some pictures
sent some pictures	;	worth more than
words	;	words
my father said	;	I hear me repeat
I won't be the father[15-8]	;	my father was
always drunk	;	blasted
my heart cracks	;	it can't hold everything
being a father	;	breaks you
the way my father was	;	the way my son will be
broken	;	broken
really is the way	;	the light gets in

15-8 *who often finds interactions with others unbearable*

(NINJAS AGAINST) THE TEMPEST OF OUR MANY TORMENTS

on my way to meet you to meet
our doctor for the last time as
hesitant as expectant as scared
so soon to be parents so I almost
miss the fist painted on the wall
a convenience store tagged with

> *ninjas against Bush*
> *hi-ya!*

my sudden laughter shakes sparrows
out of the hedge shakes a startled hop
and quickstep into the woman walking
ahead of me shakes a thought out
of my head we can use this
why not:

ninjas against poverty and hunger
ninjas against litterbugs and queue-jumpers
ninjas against traffic circles
ninjas against the home shopping channel
ninjas against both the Pope and Sinéad O'Connor
ninjas against Dutch elm disease tenth-grade

> gym the United Way Jägermeister
> *Star Trek: Voyager* prophylactic
> foam

ninjas against broken jewel case teeth green bananas
The Collected Works of T.S. Eliot the letter *K* Céline Dion
Walmart people who hate horror films Pomeranians
one-trick ponies

ninjas against puking into shopping bags in the car on
    the way to work every morning
ninjas against swelling out of your shoes shirts pants
    clothes skin patience
ninjas against baby name books life insurance and wills

ninjas against the terrifying uncertainties of genetics
    pollution food additives blind chance
ninjas against the terrifying certainties of blood[16-7] and
    bone
ninjas against knowing how much we want this
ninjas against not knowing
if we're strong enough
hi-ya

16-7 *we depend on each other because alone / we lack the*
strength

WHILE SEEKING TO IMMORTALIZE YOUR FAME

start with a list
of things you do
with your
mouth

the things you forget
when you leave
hang open like a house without a door
like a church on Monday

the things you take
when their backs are turned
creep through the walls like mice
like broken bottles

the things you promise[17-32]
at the kitchen table
hang like mosquitoes in amber
like an empty coast

the things you name
that already have names
set in early like a killing frost
like stray cats

17–32 *because indeed we really are in dire need*

the things you don't cast out
the things you bite back
the things you swallow
the things you should say but don't

sink out of sight
a hot coal in snow
dirt shovelled
down a hole

SINCE THE LORD CHASTISES US
WITH THESE WHIPS

How many times did he open the door, checking to see if
death was sneaking up on him? I often think of Galileo
this way: the plague bubbling up from the flagstones,
panic and fear burning through the city, a flea under
his microscope, fangs bared but not talking, not giving
up the genetic map. To be so close to the truth[18-34] (a
Frenchman would finally identify the plague bacteria
more than 250 years later), to know how to get the
answer but to have no time, there's never enough time,
and all around everyone else puts their faith in alchemy
and magic, and all around flowers, folk medicine.

I'm telling you now, death stalks us differently: no more
buboes or black skin sloughing off. Dead rats don't drift
against the door anymore. Everything is dying quietly
and there are too many things to believe in, too many
choices for salvation
and the flea still bares its fangs under the microscope
and I keep opening
the door.

18–34 *it is certain that when we possess this treasure / we will
fear neither danger nor death*

THE HOPE OF HAVING YOU ALWAYS NEAR
for Anya

I travel more in a week than he did in his entire life, yet my gaze remains earthbound, land-locked, a weak and stuttering imagination. Galileo was never far from his daughter, a series of concentric orbits circling her star. She never moved, spent her entire life tide-locked with her face to God.

And now I find I need a map, a chart, a Baedeker to keep track of your ever-widening ellipses.[19-35] In the hope of having you always near I'm moving less and less, following an inexorable thermodynamic spiral hoping gravity, in the end, will finally do its job.

19–35 *please remember that nothing in this world / brings me greater joy than serving you*

THAT I SHOULD BE BEGGED TO PUBLISH
SUCH A WORK
for Ty

the world is filled with motherless sons
our friends Tracy and Ian asked me to write this
they said *we want to mark our son's*
adoption with something really special
the world is filled with loneliness and fear
and children abandoned like empty bottles
like broken things
such stories to crack you wide open with grief
and Tracy and Ian step forward and pick one little boy up
the world is filled with holes empty windows
in empty houses
words thrown into falling snow
my own mother gone[20-24] so suddenly so quietly
so soon after
Tracy says *write me a poem*
the world is filled with selfless mothers
and innocent sons
and their son and my son playing like brothers the sound
of them wrapping around us filling in those spaces
those absences
that I should beg them to let me mumble these words this
welcome Ty
and thank you

20–24 *I should have to deal with fierce / foes and bitter persecu-*
tors

How Anxiously I Live,
Awaiting Word from You

I have read those letters in the box on the shelf in the
closet in the room in the apartment across the street
we got you to keep you nearer to us nearer to your new
grandchildren to keep you near

I have read your letters

like mice read the passing padding of cats
like cats read the bursting hearts of birds
like birds read the first signs of snow
like snow reads relentless gravity
like gravity reads the holes it leaves behind

I have read the holes you have left behind[21-36]

like gravity reads the snowdrifts at my door
like snow reads the drifts of nests in empty trees
like birds read the empty endless dreams of cats
like cats read the endless anxiety of mice
like mice read how anxiously I live

21–36 *this is everything / I need to tell you / for the moment*

In the Chambers of the Holy Office
Of the Inquisition

what if your life depended on your answers
what if you had already answered in writing without
knowing the questions without knowing not only your
life but your everlasting soul depended on how
you've already answered

by what means you came to Rome
did you come of your own accord
do you recognize your own words
did you know them
have you seen them since
why did Father order you to come
do you know or can you guess why you were summoned
can you explain the heavens and the elements
do you know about the earth and the sun and the order of
        the celestial spheres
did you hear what was proper to hold concerning this
        matter
do you acknowledge each and every word
do you defend teach or hold the stability of the sun
did you relate the difficulty
did you keep it in your memory
can you tell us how long
can you be specific

do you imagine the constitution of the world
do you hold it hypothetically the way Copernicus held it
is it repugnant to scripture
do you understand the complexity of the situation
do you appreciate all the nuances[22-31]
do you defend or refute the Master of the Holy Palace
did you strictly observe every order
do you know what decision was made
are you weak and inconclusive
did you use every possible care
did you seek permission
do you understand

have you testified as above
do you understand

do you?

22–31 *so as to make them lighter for you to bear*

VAINGLORIOUS AMBITION, PURE IGNORANCE, AND INADVERTENCE

better food in food courts
better reporters in *The People's Court*[23-16]
better paper for planes
better papers on planes
better peanuts in bags
better handles on luggage
better rhymes for luggage
better emotional baggage

better plugs for electric cars
better telescopes to see Mars
better light from distant stars[24-29]
better mileage for electric cars
better chocolate for candy bars
better watches on wrists
better fingers better fists
better rages

better blades on windshield wipers
better Glades for filled-up diapers
better raids for foxy swipers
better wockets in my pocketses
better cogs in pocket watches
better time with

23–16 *the impact of the emotion together*
24–29 *this truly is little or nothing*

better balls for better boys
better boys for better girls
better fathers for better children[25-12]
better mothers for better fathers

better booze in better bottles
better bums in better bars
better bars in better windows
better homes for better widows

better lead in mechanical pencils
better mechanics for southpaw pitchers
better catches and better catchers
better batter hitters
better hits and better misses
better missing

better turkeys in butter balls
better decks for X-mas halls
better gifts from Santa Claus
better Christs in Christmas
better what would Jesus do's
better makers to meet

25-12 *what matters most is the sentiment*

better nonsense than sense
better transformations
better beet plantations
better budgets for budgies
better bags for burglars
better cheese for burgers
better boogie for woogies
better buddies for Wookiees
better bitter beer faces
better snails paces
better beats per minute
better minutes for men
better mice than cats
better silk for hats
better madder hatters for tea
better sugar for me
better numbers than zeroes
better deaths for heroes
better heroes for forgetting
better forgetting for feelings

better boats for better sailing
better sailing on stiller water
better floating for Polonius's daughter[26-28]
better failures better fathers
better faith better followers
better convents better converts
better priests better popes
better beds better wards
better medicine
better endings

better forgetting

26–28 *I vex her with my constant repetition*

Faith Vested in the Miraculous Madonna of Impruneta

If there is anything that speaks to my dead mother and
her connection to her Italian father and so on up the
line through Galileo and all the way back to Cicero—
according to family lore and last name—in this entire
book it is the title of this poem

my training as a critical thinker tells me to pull this apart
word by word

my training as a poet tells me to spin out metaphor and
image word by word

my *faith* in my art tells me to just keep searching and
scratching it out word by word

my *vested in the* struggle between thought and feeling
tells me to stop writing word by word

my *miraculous* is seeing meaning in every word

my *Madonna* doesn't know what word it came from and
my *of Impruneta* can't find itself on the map

and so this poem will rest here[27-22] and weather like a
cross on an old grey church or the roses I planted on top
of the ashes I saved from the box and buried last spring
when I didn't know what else
to do

Judgment Passed on Your Book and Your Person

Galileo kneels in a church. The endless nights squinting into lens-focused aether crowd his brow. He doesn't know if the weight of his advanced years and what he's seen and calculated and written under the Holy See will ever let him stand again. It doesn't matter though because in just a moment the cardinals will announce their verdict[28-13] and condemn him to two hundred years of absurdity. As if simply saying the sun moves about the earth could make the sun move about the earth. If you look for reasons long enough you can convince yourself of anything. You can convince yourself that dogma can't beat mathematics, that your daughter hasn't wasted her life, that you survived plagues and fires for a reason, that naming Jupiter's moons for the Prince was a good idea, that there will be more wine and linen and citrus sweets, that your friends will destroy your incriminating letters, that there will be a miraculous reprieve, forgiveness, that cooler heads will prevail, that the mountains on the moon were put there for a reason, that this year's grapes will survive the early frost, that you are loved, that you haven't written your last words, that you won't be forgotten.

28–13 *the fallacy and instability of every / thing in this miserable world*

I refused him the keys
not knowing how to be older than thirteen
I gambled with not getting older than thirteen
not knowing how sheer the face was
I let the mountain slide by indestructible and complete
not knowing the finality the rush the slam of inertia
I dreamed I was a fish in the air
not knowing the cyborg touch of body and physics
        blood and mechanics
my body scaled into leather fingers which gilled the wheel
right foot finned into the speed not
knowing power steering and centripetal force I
let the camber wash me through aneled
anointed not knowing the inescapable gravity of addiction
I let him drink so I could drive not knowing
the distance of things not knowing the
force of the law not knowing my father's
accelerating pride in my adolescent manhood
not knowing the fluid the dynamic the air the rubber
the bending of light around mass[29-11]
        the inexorable cracking
frost heaving crumbling of everything we pave over
I dreamed I was a fish in the air following
this ribbon this scratch in the rock
letting the mountain slide by
indestructible and complete

29–11 *I fear that this heat may precipitate / some peculiar effect*

TERRIBLE DESTRUCTION
ON THE FEAST OF SAN LORENZO

Galileo knew, like all of you who are real Catholics know,
that this is August 10 when poor Lorenzo, the story goes,
was barbecued. "Turn me over," he apparently quipped
to his torturers, "I've cooked enough on this side." Now
that's a calendar I can get behind: ordering our days by
events, naming our lives with the titles of short stories.
What have we lost by not marking the passage of time
this way? Let's all make calendars for ourselves. I'll fill
my year with feasts for you. Every day will be a holiday
we spend in bed mapping and re-mapping ourselves
over each other. And when we're done with our days, I'll
name our hours. This is the hour of our gravity,[30-21] this
the hour of dreaming, this of breath on skin and this, and
this, and this.

30–21 *creating in me a much greater than usual / commotion of*
pleasure and happiness

RECITATION OF THE PENITENTIAL PSALMS

I worry all our songs will be lullabies and your voice
(which is the most beautiful sound I've ever heard; Bach
himself couldn't have imagined a more perfect sound)
I worry your voice will sit in the porch of my ears and
refuse to come in.

I worry we'll deviate from mathematics (which proceeds
so carefully) and so without math we'll lose logic and
momentum and without those we'll be unable to gauge
whether we've gone too far or not far enough and so it
follows that the last math we'll lose is music and then the
whole poetic bottom will fall out and all we'll be left with
are instruction manuals for machines that don't work
anymore.

I worry we'll have only four days in Spain and that on
our last day with Jacobo and his wife we'll find the place
we should have been living all this time (with orange
trees and that kind of plaster that holds light the way
Brautigan used to hold gentle glass things) and we'll look
at each other and we'll know what we need to do[31-23] but
we just won't have it in us.

31–23 *faith without works is lifeless*

I worry I won't be able to teach our children the
constellations that one midsummer night we'll look up
and not see any patterns in the stars that their ancient
light will be just that (the long-dead remnants of furnaces
now silent and cold)
and meaningless.

I worry we won't be able to keep this a secret.

I worry we'll still be piss-poor.

I worry I'll never get better at this.

I worry about the stupidest most lamest shit like will
there be enough gas in the car did I fuck up at work did I
lock the back door does this tie go with this shirt.

I worry that her death was in vain.

I worry this pen will run out of ink.

I worry this poem sucks and that this book sucks and
that I suck.

I worry that you'll read this and misunderstand.

I worry that this winter will baffle us forever that this
long grey Sunday afternoon is all we have now the
horizon between snow on the ground and snow in the
sky blurred so cold and quiet and endless.

> how do you describe a grey Sunday afternoon in winter
> all present (tense)
> no future no past

> the current frozen
> fish trapped in ice
> a plastic bag

> in a leafless tree

The Book of Life, or,
A Prophet Accepted in His Own Land

he was the first to build a proper telescope
and point it at the sky

he is the first man of the world
he will live forever in his writings
he is followed by all the best modern minds
he thinks in weights and measures and math
he is adding sand a grain at a time[32-19]

he knows that you can stitch meaning together out of
observations repeated and repeated and repeated again
with small variations introduced

he is going to keep repeating and repeating this not
because he's looking for any specific result

he is going to keep repeating and repeating this because
he's wants to see how many different results there are

he wrote books about water and memory
he softens the minutes, the seconds, the slow arc of time
he was placed and settled in the suburbs
he speaks of the shivering constellations
he caught the sun pushing through thickening air
he caught the river pouring itself through the window

32–19 *I hear that while you may have been / eclipsed or erased
briefly*

he leaves Mars behind to navigate by Jupiter
he gave me the coelacanths
he got better
he is sitting there grinning
he lies on the couch beside you
he will fit inside one of those small white holes
he will still not be still
he likes trees
he should not have taken so much
he took some pictures
he is against not knowing
he is the things you name
he knows how to get the answer
he remains earthbound
he was thrown into falling snow
he reads relentless gravity
he can explain the heavens and the elements
he catches better batters
he will rest here and weather
he outlived two hundred years of absurdity
he knows the distance of things
he cooked enough
he used to hold gentle glass things
he faced the moon
he held your sound

he taught us to fish

My Soul and Its Longing

tide by tide locked I revolve
around it like that
which drives the moon[33–14]
a lunatic engine
arranging and rearranging
battering all the available data
to no end
my reason is weak and untrue
broken   blown   burned
I am enthralled

33–14 *because desire makes me hope / that you must soon arrive*

UNTIL I HAVE THIS FROM YOUR LIPS
after Charles Bernstein

every lip has a mouth every mouth
a face by face mouth by mouth
every lip has a girl every girl
a day by day girl by girl
every lip has a sound every sound
a story by story sound by sound
every lip has two every two
a four two by four by two I'll
build you a house to hold your
days your face your lips
every lip has a revelation
every revelation a swelling belly
every belly a baby I'll build
you a house to hold your face
your mouth I'll build you a
house to hold your sound your
story your word baby falling
from your lips I'll build[34-18]
our baby a house when I
hear the word from your mouth
your lips

34–18 *so my sudden joy was as great / as it was unexpected*

As I Struggle to Understand
for Carmela

as to do otherwise would be to injure yourself
I am more than a little bit curious

as I could not imagine how to begin
I am filled with apprehension and fear

as through your most gentle and loving letters
we can calm our anxious spirits

as I have no one else in this world who can console me
I grieve over your departure

as we must patiently submit ourselves to the will[35-9]
I suspect that he is complaining about us

as it is impossible for so many brains to be of one mind
they then carry us in their mouths

as an extraordinary thing to ask of people living so far away
this particular failing of mine

as I abandon myself to thoughts of you
I thank you for the fish

as working outdoors has done you considerable harm
I implore you to leave the garden to its own devices

35–9 *now that it has arrived at this stage*

as I derive delight simply from beholding them
such apples are an extraordinary thing in this cold season

as between the infinite love I bear you and my fear of this
sudden cold
I worry that this separation will be a long one

as the general state of human misery
is perfect happiness

as I have read thus far without stopping
I must interrupt to ask whether this is indeed true

as I am enjoying this more as poetry
I know all this proves nothing ·

as wishing above all else to have news of you
as only to hear a word carried from your lips
as you tolerate all of this vexation with such patience
as I have searched everywhere to find you
as the hot weather that oppresses us
as we are burdened by penury and poverty
as the day does not contain one hour of time that is ours
as our sorrow at losing   her   is

in order to live as quietly as possible
the darkness of the winter
provokes some fear in me

THE MEMORY OF THE SWEETNESSES

the first night after
we first found out
our first night as
almost mom soon-
to-be dad
like our first time together[36-1]
that first night alone
we fumbled towards each
other not knowing where
to put our hands not
knowing how to wrap our
bodies around each other
and the first child growing
inside you between us
that first night we held
our hands we held
that night we held
that first sweet night

36–1 *he had in mind a great quantity of poetry*

(Or Move Within It)

In the present small treatise I set forth some matters of great interest for all observers of natural phenomena to look at and consider. They are of great interest, I think, first, from their intrinsic excellence; secondly, from their absolute novelty; and lastly, also on account of the instrument by the aid of which they have been presented to my apprehension.

—Galileo

The poems that follow are an invitation. Part of the title of Galileo's treatise *Bodies That Stay Atop Water is (or move within it)*. Similarly, throughout the preceding section of this book, footnotes live and move within the main text, and in this next section, these footnotes (and the text they apply to) are brought forward as the bodies, the meaning, that moves within the book. This is a space for you to gather, collate, and interpret both the footnotes themselves and the text that is footnoted to create new poems. The final appearance of these poems will depend on which of the two numbers in each footnote notation you use to order your text. To get you started, two possible poems follow.

Poem "1" assumes that the footnote notation refers to the text in the footnotes at the bottom of the page. The slashes in the footnotes indicate line breaks and while these lines are randomly arranged in poem 1, they don't have to be. These lines may speak to you another way and you are free to arrange them in any order you want.

Poem "2" assumes that the footnote notation refers to the line in the poem which is footnoted. This poem also assumes that the lines are meant to be placed in sequence according to the second number of the footnote and are arranged as such. Though I've used footnoted lines in their entirety in some places, in others, I've taken some creative license and used only a few words. Again, you are free and encouraged to choose whichever words you like.

So what if these lines were arranged in numerical order by the first number in the notation rather than the second? What would happen if you took these lines, this data, and arranged them in a contrary order? What if you chose to assume that the footnote numbers referred to the line following the number rather than the line preceding it? What would the results be? Would this uncover truths previously obscured? You are encouraged to experiment and poems "3" and "4" have been left blank specifically for this purpose. Go ahead, read with pen in hand, write in the book, rearrange it. And if you discover something particularly interesting that you'd like to share, please send it to me at paul. pearson@me.com. With your permission, I will post your results on lunaticengine.com so anyone is who interested can test their hypotheses against the data—just like Galileo taught us.

1

he had in mind a great quantity of poetry
he was sure that many more existed
which were not only unknown
but unimaginable
so beautifully written
that they have only kindled
my desire to see more
an extraordinary thing in this cold season

I think you will be much pleased with it
though I know that your joy must be
tainted with considerable sorrow
we depend on each other because alone
we lack the strength
who often finds interactions with others unbearable
now that it has arrived at this stage
until there shall be given to us the true
constitution of the parts of the universe

I fear that this heat may precipitate
some peculiar effect
what matters most is the sentiment
the fallacy and instability of every
thing in this miserable world

because desire makes me hope
that you must soon arrive
so my sudden joy was as great
as it was unexpected
seeing the splendor of the sun and the stars
the impact of the emotion together
could drink in this universal power and authority

I hear that while you may have been
eclipsed or erased briefly
creating in me a much greater than usual
commotion of pleasure and happiness
obliging me to hide in silence
so that this ship can bring itself safely into port

I fear this activity will do you harm

I should have to deal with fierce
foes and bitter persecutors
who appreciate the true significance of their calling
so as to make them lighter for you to bear
by living in obedience
without anything of one's own
and in chastity
this rule is never broken
this truly is little or nothing
since we are all of us here on Earth like strangers

I vex her with my constant repetition

because indeed we really are in dire need
faith without works is lifeless
it is certain that when we possess this treasure
we will fear neither danger nor death
please remember that nothing in this world
brings me greater joy than serving you
this is everything
I need to tell you
for the moment

2

like our first time together
by this experience
made up
like tree swallows
the moon's penumbra
a new fetish
the terrifying certainties of blood
I won't be the father
as we must patiently submit ourselves to the will
your soon-to-be swelling belly waiting
the bending of light around mass
better fathers for children
the cardinals will announce their verdict
which drives the moon
the wisdom of the patriarchs degrades
in *The People's Court*
speak of my father
from your lips I'll build
adding sand a grain at a time
the quality of miracles isn't what it used to be
this is the hour of our gravity
and so this poem will rest here
we'll know what we need to do
my own mother gone
those small white holes
I could be a monkey
I don't see the sun
for Polonius's daughter

light from distant stars
I hear in your words
all the nuances
the things you promise
like a fist in the mouth
to be so close to the truth
your ever-widening ellipses
the holes you have left behind

3

4

BAEDEKER

[S]ince she well understood that all human monuments do perish at last by violence, by weather, or by age, she took a wider view, and invented more imperishable signs, over which destroying Time and envious Age could claim no rights ....

—Galileo

The Last Lost

like him I want to put the stars
in their proper places
to stop this wandering
to be sure
to be fixed

a simple orbit becomes a chaos
of circles connected on sticks
pulled by unseen works of gear and axle
and simple machines made un-simple
a grinding orrery instead of smooth
mathematical motion

the simplest of exhortations fail
stacks of sacred texts built on the same
golden foundation crumbling
catechesis used as a pickaxe
the rubble weaponized

what chance do the rest of us stand when not
only the works of God but the word of God
is subject to Entropy

I need a map of all our maladies
a Baedeker of the violence
we've been given
we have to name them
what else can we do

10

the first violence seethes like no other
all violence that follows shifts on the
uneasy sandstone of that first murder
the surprise at snaring your first
gopher after dozens of tries
hundreds of knots in fishing line
the sudden momentum of the situation
Jordan cheering you on and greedy and jealous
of the dollar its tail will get you while you
watch the thing thrash in the noose
you made twisting to breathe turning itself
over and over in mid-air

then done

now in the stillness take the knife lay the
limp thing on a rock and try to take the tail
with one stroke try to make it clean try
not to squeeze it then splash vomit over the bloody mess

now stay out of the bush you don't
belong here

EUROPA

this violence just won't end there's so much saltwater
the surface of this hurt won't stay frozen

you wrote a poem twenty years ago
not long after it happened
called "behind your apartment"
it was a long collection of short images
from behind her apartment where you'd smoke

the dumpster the stray cat the yellow paint
parking lines chipped on wet pavement
and the searing anger at your complete powerlessness
to stop what happened
the dirt-eating anger
the realization the absolute fundamental knowledge
that you couldn't stop it from happening again

so you wrote a poem and shared it with her
that last night before she closed the door she said
"now you've raped me"
she said "I've been raped again"
and the second violence was brought home
like a hammer coming down on your head
like the way she raised her hand
and let it fall again

GANYMEDE

you marble you magnificent
you most beautiful of mortals
what have you done?
you metallic you muscled
you horse you eagle
you lightning bolt of beauty
you think this is not violence?
that you would remain inviolate?
insoluble in the tide of ten thousand days?
this is the cliff this is the turning this
is the singular point of knowing as
you hold this new life for the first time
knowing now you're not immortal
you've placed the better share of you
into this infant this eternal youth
what you have known as you
will slowly empty and crumble
you marble you magnificent
Parthenon

CALLISTO

and if this wasn't enough
she lies in that room there
down the hall and you

think instead about her cats
who can you get to take her cats

cold feet her feet are so cold
you can't believe a body
could be so cold it's not
a body then only marble
your mother turning to marble
starting at the feet

the cats are old twins two
presences there is not one
without the other

you know

she won't wake
her eyes are
closed
this waiting is just formality
politeness

the smaller cat is sick
has stopped eating
the other just looks at it
and doesn't understand

you know you should
say goodbye but you can't
you're in a frieze
your entire narrative
is carved out along
the wall between this waiting
room and her final bed

both the sick cat
and the other are alone
in her apartment waiting
not looking at each other

and so you know the final violence
the refusal to witness

BIBLIOGRAPHY

For in him we live, and move, and have our being; as certain also of your own poets have said, For we are also his offspring.

—Acts 17:28

But let us proceed a little farther, and observe ....

—Galileo

THE LITTLE BALANCE

*Lowborn men are but a breath, the highborn are but a lie; if
weighed on a balance, they are nothing; together they are only a
breath.*

—Psalms 62:9

*Let me speak first of the surface of the Moon, which is turned
towards us.*

—Galileo

how many times did these stars rise unnoticed
flickering back and forth in their orbits
since before the seas were parted from the land
these wandering stars waiting for someone
to look up

think about the moment when it dawned
on him that he was the first human to see
these moons the first to know that other
planets had other satellites
imagine how he smiled

the temptation to self-name them must have been strong:
Galileo 1
Galileo 2
Galileo 3
Galileo 4

at least they're not called:
Medici 1
Medici 2
Medici 3
Medici 4

flippancy aside
how do you name the first new thing since the Fall
try to tip the scale to redress the fact
that a common mathematician pierced the primum mobile
by attributing the ability the grace to your prince

why name them at all
Galileo and Medici are but words
and words but broken wind
to misquote

but moons swinging around a distant planet
an immediate devastating rupture in
the nature of reality from one moment to the next
in a blink resolved in ground glass
the modern age was born

faced with new moons
one must only try to remember
to breathe

ON MOTION

At this also my heart trembleth, and is moved out of his place.

—Job 37:1

[O]r I will prove that the Earth has motion, and surpasses the Moon in brightness ....

—Galileo

that which chases clouds before it like wolves on sheep

that which flings salmon upstream as an aquatic singularity

that which maps invisible cities into memory from books we've only read

that which sparks, flares, and disappears in the first immeasurable instant after the switch is thrown

that which sits as potential energy on the contrapuntal cliffs separating Bach's Partitas from Bach's Cantatas

that which turns water into beer

that which eats momentum leaving only heat

that which then eats that heat

that which foxes hear through snow

that which keeps deer mice alive through winter

that which is reflected in your eyes when you think of home

that which is spiralled and spun into every living cell

that which keeps bodies atop water

that which keeps me moving within it

that which named the days

that which gets lonely

that which sits above the plane of the ecliptic

that which the camera captures

that which the paintbrush calls into light

that which applies torque

that which measures camber

that which invented the words torque and camber and left them here for me to use that which has written out the equations to describe the quantum cloud of charge and probability that surrounds every moment

that which has measured out our small slice of time

that which sits across from you now

that which breathes

that which knows you too well

that which will see you in death

that which moves through all things

that which doesn't move

that which moves all things

MECHANICS

She is more precious than rubies: and all the things thou canst
desire are not to be compared to her.

—Proverbs 3:15

[A]nd what Experiment teacheth us ....

—Galileo

what can be known by watching one body
pass in front of another by passing
your body in front of mine

what can be extrapolated by knowing the sun
is a gong ringing in the airless aether impossible music
trapped in stained glass

what can be assumed by putting bodies into water
measuring how much water moves like crossing
water onto bodies measuring what that body moves

what can be described by dropping things from towers
counting until they either hit or don't

keep counting because
what can be halved can be halved again
the distance between two gravities
geometrically reducing the distance between us

what can be measured by passing
our bodies back and forth each time we come
too close we inscribe fractal patterns of desire
into the very air reaching out half the distance
between us and half again falling towards an
inevitable mathematical consummation

The Starry Messenger

He that hath ears to hear, let him hear.

—Matthew 11:15

Again, it is a most beautiful and delightful sight to behold the body of the Moon ....

—Galileo

what did you come up here to see?
the shivering reed is a stick in frozen mud
this northern prairie may look like it is laid
in a soft robe of snow but the sleep it calls
you to will last well past spring
the only royalty here are the magpies
strutting in their iridescent vestments
they are made of ice
you are not

and later the moon
the borealis writhing
wreathing advent
the night shivering
rampant with stars

but it is the silence
that moves you
a silence so violent
you can hear at last

DISCOURSE ON FLOATING BODIES

And the man of God said, Where fell it? And he shewed him the place. And he cut down a stick, and cast it thither; and the iron did swim.

—2 Kings 6:6

These things explained and proved, I come to consider that which offers it self ....

—Galileo

and then there's the story of the strange kid next door
who would spend all afternoon staring at the river
said he saw something in the ice
just there not a fish not a stick not a stone

said he could see it when he closed his eyes
said he'd dream about it
said it was an angel trapped in the ice
that if we waited until it got dark then we would see it too
said the January sun was too bright
moonlight was needed

of course they didn't let him out at night
he'd just sit staring out the window at the snow
said he could see it with his eyes closed
said it was calling out to him

imagine all those January nights spent staring
knowing an angel is just
there
through the woods just
past the last streetlights
on the other side of the highway
down there
by the snowbanks
trapped in swirling black ice

he must have gotten so tired of not being believed
that look in all our eyes
he just stopped talking
would look through people
as if they weren't there
trying to help him
staring towards the river

everyone knew it was only a matter of time before the
night his parents ran panicked and screaming down the
street leading a growing crowd of neighbours through
the park across the highway through the close white
shivering pines and down the steep snowbanked banks

and there's their strange kid spread-eagle on the ice
he's cleaned a patch of snow away with his arms and legs
the ink black river is flowing in its last narrow unfrozen
channel not far from him

and he's spread out in the sandy moonlight tapping on
the ice with a stick trying to free that angel when of
course the ice suddenly cracks not like wings radiating
out from his body but like an axe
snapping bone

and in that brief moment as the strange kid slips under
we can all finally
see

LETTERS ON SUNSPOTS

And for the precious fruits brought forth by the sun, and for the
precious things put forth by the moon.

—Deuteronomy 33:14

I ask you to give him this piece of news from me; that I have
most conclusive arguments ready, showing clearly that, just as
he holds, all the planets receive their light from the sun, being by
constitution bodies dark and devoid of light ....

—Galileo

and as we sit in April and wait
for the days to grow longer we think
of other things we can measure:

the height of the tiny seeds
just sprouted in the tiny pots
lined up on the kitchen sill

the number of times your thumb has played
middle C this past week while learning the national anthem
so you can play it in front of the whole school
at the year-end concert in June

the length of time it takes
for the sun to travel from one end
of the cat to the other

the approximate distance our afternoon snack of bananas
travelled by hand by donkey by truck by ship by truck again
by our car and at last by hand again to our mouths

the ratio between your six years and your forty-two
inches of height and your thirty
centimetres of hair and your five
missing teeth

and you say there aren't numbers large enough
to measure how much you love me

I am undone by you daughter and your
terrible host of hugs and kisses

though even the sun is blemished
in this season in this moment
you are perfect
my dove
my undefiled one

DISCOURSE ON THE TIDES
*It is the glory of God to conceal a thing: but the honour of kings
is to search out a matter.*

—Proverbs 25:2

*But though he hath exquisitely Philosophiz'd, in investigating
the solution of the doubts he proposeth, yet will I not undertake
to maintain, rather various difficulties, that present themselves
unto me, give me occasion of suspecting that he hath not entirely
displaid unto us, the true Cause of the present Conclusion ....*

—Galileo

so then let Thomas be our captain now that we've finally
asked the question outright

he's the one who put his hand into the hole in the sea and
poked the impossible animals left behind in pools like
shallow graves

when the sea is rolled away, when the scales of water have
fallen from the shore, Thomas says he feels fine

he knows it is not a love of earth that keeps us crawling
around beneath the sun

he knows evolution does not progress from lower to
higher but from life to death

he knows that like water, all things are seeking their true
place

he knows the North Star is not the brightest star

he knows there is no dark side of the moon

he knows the five second rule is bullshit

he knows the memory centre of the brain grows new cells
by converting memories of the Fall to blank slates

he knows that a penny dropped from heaven is not fatal,
at least not immediately

he knows that the heat and light of a meteor comes from
the compressed air it is pushing as it falls, that it takes
more than our thin skin of air to melt the cold from the
journey through space

he knows that lightning strikes twice and strikes tall
things again for good measure

he knows there is gravity in space, there is gravity
everywhere

he knows that *Brontosaurus* never existed, that adding
salt to water won't make it boil faster, that goldfish have
good memories, that cockroaches won't survive the
holocaust

that warm milk won't help you sleep

he knows the sun is not on fire

he knows the stars do not twinkle

he knows speed and velocity are not interchangeable and
neither are weight and mass

he knows a duck's quack echoes

he knows a bird won't abandon its babies if you touch
them any more than you would abandon your babies if a
bird touched them

bats are not blind
houseflies can live for a month
sunflowers don't track the sun

he knows we have more than five senses
he knows balance, acceleration, and pain
he knows the core of the earth is a solid ball
of nickel and iron

he knows Galileo did not invent the telescope
he knows Copernicus was not the first person to place
the sun at the centre

he knows correlation does not imply causation

he knows it is not the seas that keep the moon in place
but he also knows that the moon is the
engine of our desire
and he knows that in zero-G
this gravity well is but one
more
tidal pool

Discourse on the Comets

Raging waves of the sea, foaming out their own shame; wander-
ing stars, to whom is reserved the blackness of darkness forever.
                                        —Jude 1:13

[A]gain inviting the attention of all who are eager for true philos-
ophy to the beginnings which led to the sight of most important
phenomena.
                                        —Galileo

Galileo once wrote that comets were merely vapours
let off by the earth shimmering between the moon
and our eyes a flame seen through an oily fingerprint
on a half-empty glass

You will be known for what you believe
I should know where this is going but I don't

I remember once seeing the northern lights through a
dirty and foggy car window lying in the backseat with my
pants around my ankles an art history major who doesn't
remember me anymore lying on top of me with her
pants around her ankles the angle just right green gauzy
curtains of star stuff streaming her hair moving back and
forth into focus and out the aurora washing over her bare
shoulder

Do you remember once saying that you'd never fall in
love again?

I should know where this is going by now but I don't

And then there are the Perseids packing the kids into
the car threading our way down lightless gravel roads to
find a dry field sitting in the swarming night glimpsing
bats through clouds of mosquitoes three years it took to
get clear skies deep enough into the night to see the flash
the bright streaking death of an aeons-old bit of dust
undeniable evidence striking my children like a hammer
between the eyes

What did Luke say about recognizing what our eyes have
seen? And I still don't know where this is going

Have we done enough to make ourselves believe that
Halley's Comet is coming back now that we know better
how to look up a thousand thousand stars wink back at
us occluded by planets we didn't believe in my father said
that I'd want to tell my kids how I saw Halley's where I
was who I was with I was sixteen I didn't believe him and
now a new planet is discovered almost every day new
mathematics describe the subtle surprising geometry of
space proving that a photon of light travels through every
point on its trajectory simultaneously and while light is
everywhere at once most of the universe is made up of
dark matter we can't detect so the metaphor that we're
all bright stars wandering in the dark turns out to be
scientifically as well as scripturally true

the kingdom of God can
only come
through careful observation

I should know how to end this by now but I don't

No matter which vocabulary we use to describe it the
one thing we all fear is that we are really alone no matter
which tool we use so look up look waaaaay up whether
with wine or poetry or virtue whether with science
or religion or art one must always be like a drunken
boat floating in a sea of stars bright sparks wandering
beautifully alone together forever

THE ASSAYER

*Who hath measured the waters in the hollow of his hand, and
meted out heaven with the span, and comprehended the dust of
the earth in a measure, and weighed the mountains in scales,
and the hills in a balance?*

—Isaiah 40:12

*At the first hour of the next night I saw these heavenly bodies
arranged in this manner ....*

—Galileo

mitochondria are tiny dragonflies
that live in the smallest parts of us
feeding by freeing the energy
stored in their shimmering wings

E. coli swarm our guts
like termites in a rotten log
breaking all the shit we have to eat
every day down into little somethings greater than
the sum of them

Demodex reach across the gap
of our eyelids while we sleep
wrap their arms around each
other sealing the windows
of our eyes against the night
mares that push against us
until we rip them apart
in the morning
like Velcro

we burn from the inside with the light
of a million million mycobacterial candles
ulcers, tuberculosis, leprosy
the entire tragic rotting of human history
blossoms in their guttering smoke

we destroy everything we touch and everything
we touch destroys us one cell at a time
we're each hosting our own personal
titanomachia throwing up new cells
as fast as they are brought down

we shuffle through our lives a roiling sloughing mass
a continually breaking down negotiation
between reason and entropy
a necrotic parliament of squabbling
biomass

what grows on what we leave behind
what gods our bodies spawn

Discourses and Mathematical Demonstrations Relating to Two New Sciences

So teach us to number our days, that we may apply our hearts unto wisdom.

—Psalms 90:12

But let it suffice for the present to have thus slightly touched, and as it were just put our lips to these matters ....

—Galileo

Saint Fibonacci is counting the number of times I've gone around the immovable centre of all these words. He knows the means of gold, the atomic weight of things, knows what the little difference is, the philosopher's stone, the philosophic mercury, the vital agent, the latent spirit, the subtle spirit, the secret fire, the material soul of matter, the invisible inhabitant, the seed, the seminal virtue, the body of light, the unseen engine of mechanical and vegetable motion. He sits at the head of the combined hagiography, Saint Mandelbrot on his right, Saint Augustine on his left. Matter and the immaterial are met together, experiment and sacrament have kissed and all the tongues and gods of Babel are brought back together all describing the same indescribable infinite

0,1, 1, 2, 3, 5, 8, 13, 21, 34, 55, 89 ...

ad infinitum

Acknowledgements

My first and foremost gratitude goes to my family: my wife Suzanne and my children Oscar and Anya who put up with me scrawling in notebooks in the interstices of our lives for so many years. Thanks to my brother David, Sulu to my Chekov—or is it the other way around? And of course, thanks to my mother, Carmela, who is no longer with us, and my father, Wally.

I am forever indebted to friends and colleagues Andy Weaver, Jonathan Meakin, Todd Babiak, Doug Barbour, Wendy McGrath and so many others. Shawna Lemay, Kimmy Beach, and Peter Midgley all offered insightful advice and encouragement as this thing came together. I am lucky to live in such a vibrant, supportive literary community. From the Stroll of Poets, tireless advocates of poetry for everyone, to Olive Editors past and present, I have had the privilege of knowing and working with so many amazing people!

I owe deep thanks to everyone at Turnstone Press, with whom it has been a true pleasure to work and whose support of this project humbles me. And finally, special thanks to Alice Major who, in addition to being a friend for almost twenty years, was the final mechanic on this engine.

Earlier versions of some poems in this collection have previously appeared in other publications including *Peter F. Yacht Club*, *Event*, *Wonk*, and the anthology *Writing the Land: Alberta Through Its Poets*.

REFERENCES

This book would not have been possible without two won-
derful books by Dava Sobel: *Galileo's Daughter* (Penguin
Books Limited, 1999) from which the titles of the poems
in the "Bodies That Stay Atop Water" section are taken;
and *Letters to Father* (Penguin Books Limited, 2001). They
are used with permission.

The lines in one of the two footnote poems have also
been taken from both *Galileo's Daughter* and *Letters to
Father*, at whim. Again, I must thank Ms. Sobel deeply
and sincerely and beg her forgiveness for taking such lib-
erties with her perfect text. Again these lines are used with
permission.

The epigraphs quoting Galileo are all taken from either
The Sidereal Messenger of Galileo Galilei, a translation
with introduction and notes by Edward Stafford Carlos
(Rivingtons, 1880), or *A Discourse Presented to the Most
Serene Don Cosimo II. Great Duke of Tuscany: Concerning
The Natation of Bodies Upon, or Submersion In, the Water*
translated by Thomas Salusbury, ESQ. (William Leybourn,
1663). Both were accessed via Project Gutenberg at
https://www.gutenberg.org/ebooks/46036 and https://
www.gutenberg.org/ebooks/37729, respectively and are
in the public domain.

The epigraphs quoting scripture are all from *The Holy
Bible: King James Version.*

The epigraph for the "Abstract" section is from
"Instructions for preparing an initial manuscript." *Science*,
American Association for the Advancement of Science,